# CFA 2026: Level 1 corporate Issuers

## CFA level 1, Volume 1

M. Imran Ahsan

Published by M. Imran Ahsan, 2020.

CFA 2026: LEVEL 1 CORPORATE ISSUERS

**First edition. May 10, 2020.**



ISBN: 979-8224569625

Written by M. Imran Ahsan.

# Also by M. Imran Ahsan

**ACCA**
ACCA: Business & Technology


**CFA level 1**
CFA 2026: Level 1 corporate Issuers
CFA Level 1 Financial Statement Analysis
CFA level 1: 2025 Equity Investments
CFA 2025: Level 1 Fixed Income
Economics for CFA 2024: level 1 in just one week
CFA Level 1: Derivatives and Alternative Investments
CFA 2025: level 1 Portfolio management


**Investment series**
Corporate Finance: A Beginner's Guide
Fixed Income Securities: A Beginner's Guide to Understand, Invest and
Evaluate Fixed Income Securities


**Personal Finance**

Side Hustle Success: Unlock Your Earning Potential

Side Hustle Success: Unlock Your Earning Potential

To all those aspirants who are eager to learn more with the least effort.

# CFA 2026: Level 1
# Corporate Issuers

## Complete in just 1-week

Dr. M. Imran Ahsan Dhothar

Dedicated to all smart Learners

Successful people ask better questions, and as a result, they get better answers.

Tony Robins

# Preface

Are you looking to navigate the intricate details of Corporate Issuers for CFA level 1 2026 within a constrained timeline? This brief guide is specifically crafted for that purpose. This book thoroughly addresses all the essential topics, providing clear and concise explanations along with practical examples where necessary. We aim to assist you in optimizing your study efforts and attaining the best score achievable. Professional Insights: The material is crafted by seasoned expert with a profound knowledge of the curriculum. Through commitment and efficient study techniques, you can approach the corporate issuers section of the exam with assurance. This book serves as your guide to achieving success. Wishing you all the best!

Dr. M. Imran Ahsan Dhothar

Feel free to contact Ch.imranahsen@gmail.com

M. IMRAN AHSAN

# Learning module 1
# Organizational Forms, Corporate Issuer Features, and Ownership

**1: Compare the organizational forms of businesses**

For a group to reach a goal, it needs to be organized. The organization could be a company, a non-profit, the government, or a school. Structures, jobs and duties are what make up organizations. They have a reason for doing what they're doing, goals, and aims. In groups, people use their skills and put in their time to help the group. For teamwork to work, people need to be able to coordinate and talk to each other. Organizations need things like money, technology, and people to work. They follow the rules and laws that are in place. Each group has its own culture and set of beliefs. They need to be able to deal with changes in the world. Groups of people work together to complete tasks, and they have a big effect on society, business, and government.

A business organization is a group of people who work together to give customers goods or services in exchange for money. It can be a business that is run to make money, like a company or a shop. Organizations in business have a set framework and clear goals they want to reach. To do their work, they need things like money, tools, and people to work for them. A business's main goal is to meet the needs and wants of its customers while also making money and getting a profit.

All groups can be split up into smaller parts called subsystems. For instance, a business has sections like manufacturing, sales and marketing, and accounts. It's possible to split each section into even smaller parts. For example, the bookkeeping department has several sub-departments, such as cash, accounts, payables, and ledgers.

**Close system/ close organizations**: The name "closed systems" comes from the fact that these systems don't talk to other systems. There isn't much to these methods, and they don't last long. If a business doesn't pay attention to new technologies, competition, and customer wants, it will have a hard time succeeding.

**Open system/ Open organizations:** "Open organizations" do affect their surroundings. They take in information from their surroundings and send it back out into the world. The ones that are useful and important in the real world are these open platforms.

**Types of organizations**

**Commercial Organizations:** Companies whose primary goal is to increase their financial wealth are known as commercial organizations. Different legal structures are available for them, such as partnerships, limited liability partnerships, sole proprietorships, and limited liability corporations. In the event of financial trouble and liquidation, owners are better protected by limited liability partnerships and limited businesses. The owners are shielded from personal responsibility and creditors may only seize the company's assets in such a scenario. But partners and sole proprietors are personally liable for all company obligations to an infinite extent.

**Commercial organizations are typically classified into different sectors:**

**Primary vs secondary sector:** Resource extraction and processing are at the heart of the primary sector.

In the secondary sector, production is the main emphasis.

Offering products and services is what the tertiary sector looks for.

In some instances, a quaternary sector is distinguished, which includes R&D businesses like pharmaceutical and information technology.

**Non-profit organizations:** The not-for-profit sector is another category of organizations. Charities, including nonprofit medical centers, exemplify a not-for-profit organization. Their accounting system is based on revenue and expenses rather than profit and loss. To stay afloat, non-profits must ensure that their revenue is more than or equal to their expenditures.

**Public sector organizations**: Public sector organizations are owned by the government, either on a federal or state level. The military, healthcare, and school systems are all examples of organizations that fall within the umbrella of the public sector. In some countries, the government may have a stake in other sectors of the economy, such as national airlines. Even while nonprofits may have a business motive, but that's not always the case.

**NGOs:** NGOs, or non-governmental organizations, are groups that work globally and are usually not for profit. This group includes a large number of United Nations agencies.

**Cooperatives:** All people who work for a cooperative own a piece of it. As an example, in order to sell their goods better, farmers may form cooperatives. In cooperatives, members work together to achieve a common goal—the pursuit of profits—while also sharing in the ownership of the business.

**Organization structures**

Different types of organizational structures can be categorized as follows:

- Entrepreneurial
- Functional
- Divisional
- Matrix
- Boundary-less

Organizational structures can be classified into several categories, including entrepreneurial, functional, divisional, matrix, and boundary-less structures.

**Entrepreneurial structure:** The most basic kind of an entrepreneurial organization is a manager and an employee team. Typically, these firms are tiny and operated by families. As a result, they don't need distinct divisions. Many times, the same persons serve as both owners and managers. A **functional structure is** often adopted when a simple company grows. Sales and marketing, accounting, payments, receivables, and R&D are just a few examples of the functions that can benefit from their own dedicated department. This organizational setup may be very successful because each department is free to concentrate on what it does best, which in turn reduces overhead costs.

The main tasks in an organization can be grouped into different functions:

- Ordering and purchasing: This involves buying materials and assets from suppliers.
- Manufacturing/production: Creating goods that customers want to buy.
- Direct service provision: Providing specialized services like legal, accounting, or consulting work.
- Sales and marketing: Finding and selling to customers.
- Distribution: Getting products to customers, often through outside companies.
- Administration: Handling office tasks and record-keeping.
- Research and development: Creating new products or ways of making things.
- Human resources: Hiring, training, and managing employees.
- Accounting and finance: Dealing with payments, invoices, and financial statements.
- Cash and working capital management: Managing money and ensuring enough to pay bills and expenses.
- Treasury management: The treasury department is essential to every large company's financial management system. Capital needs, issuing more shares, getting loans from banks, and figuring out dividend payments are all key aspects that they evaluate. They are also concerned with reducing interest rates and foreign currency risk. Another part is lowering the company's tax obligations, which has been a gripe for many

famous businesses.

As businesses expand, a clear delineation between shareholders as owners, a board of directors as decision-makers, and managers as implementers of board decisions becomes more apparent. This is called a **divisional structure**. Separating a company into subsets according to goods or locations could be useful if it keeps growing. Because every department deals with unique production, markets, competition, and laws, this setup enables them to focus on what they do best.

**Matrix systems** are more sophisticated. Imagine a collective project. Assume Project A has a project team and manager. Team members do work for this boss. For instance, one project manager may handle money and another quality control. Someone may also manage project workers. In a matrix firm, each employee manages projects and functions.

Each worker in a matrix firm reports to two individuals. They report to the project manager and department heads. This approach may appear harsh to conventional managers, but it's the realities and expectations of workers. Managers collaborate better using the grid framework. If Project B is behind schedule, Project B and Quality Control managers may collaborate to speed up quality control. After selecting a repair, quality control may implement it.

**A boundaryless** organization can take different forms:

Virtual: Creating a separate company outside the main organization to seize temporary market opportunities.

Hollow: Outsourcing non-core operations like accounting, human resources, legal services, and manufacturing allows the company to focus on its core strengths, such as designing new products.

Modular: Ordering components from various internal and external providers and assembling them into a final product.

**5. Mintzberg's structures**

Mintzberg divides organizations into five. Strategic apex—top management or the Board of Directors—is the first phase. Second is the middle line, where intermediate managers convey orders down the organization. The third portion is the operational core, which comprises daily workers. Fourth are support personnel like accounting and IT. Tec structure creates and enforces standards and processes like quality control manuals and employee handbooks.

These sections of the organization vary in size and significance each organization. A tiny entrepreneurial company has a strategy apex, functioning core, and little middle line, support personnel, and technostructure. A major accounting or law firm's middle line is shorter, reflecting a tighter interaction between the partners at the top and the audit or legal staff. Support personnel is large, but the technostructure is tiny. Standardized processes are less appropriate in these organizations since they personalize solutions to specific customers.

In summary, organizations have five parts: strategic apex, middle line, operational core, support personnel, and technostructure. These sections differ per organization in size and significance. Due to client-specific solutions, professional organizations have a shorter middle line and smaller technostructure.

## 6. Levels

Organizations are often seen as having three levels tactical, operational, and strategic. These levels are called the "Anthony hierarchy". The board of directors and the top managers make up the strategic level, which is at the very top. As part of their primary job, they may make plans for the next five years as part of the organization's long-term strategy. In order to follow this plan, the business needs to decide where it will be based and whether it will switch from making things to offering services.

At the very bottom is the operational level, which is where daily tasks are carried out. Most of the jobs on this level are short-term and can be finished in one day. Planning doesn't take long—usually just one or two weeks. At this level, people's main job is to carry out deals or keep track of them. This means they write bills, handle orders, and answer customer questions.

In the middle is the tactical level, which is made up of area heads. The managers are busy making sure the budget and goals for the year are met, so they only have a year to make plans. They are also in charge of daily jobs, but their main goal is to set up their area to fit the year's budget and goals.

### 7. Tall/narrow, wide/flat

Organizations can be categorized as either tall-narrow or wide-flat. In a tall-narrow structure, each manager or supervisor has a relatively small number of subordinates, indicating a "span of control." On the other hand, in a wide-flat structure, the span of control is much broader.

In a tall-narrow organization, there are many hierarchical layers, and due to the small number of subordinates, there is close supervision. This type of structure is often described as bureaucratic, formal, and focused on strict job descriptions and grades. In contrast, a wide-flat organization is more egalitarian, with less hierarchy and greater communication between top and bottom levels. There is less emphasis on strict job descriptions and more focus on teamwork and getting the job done.

Many organizations consciously switched from tall-narrow to wide-flat buildings in the 1990s via "delayering" or "flattening." Two key variables caused this transition. First, cheaper Far Eastern manufacturing countries put pressure on costs. Western companies have to simplify processes and remove middle-man jobs to compete. Second, rapid technical improvements and worldwide market shifts required quicker organization responses. Multiple layers and resistance to change made the tall-narrow construction hard to adapt; therefore, wide-flat structures were used for agility and flexibility.

It is important to note that the term "scalar chain" refers to the hierarchical chain of command within a company, from the top to the bottom.

## 8. Centralization / Decentralization

Organizational structure and power are different. Two organizations with the same form might have differing authority for different employee ranks. Centralization or decentralization determines organizational power distribution. Decentralization may be useful or harmful.

Many benefits come from decentralization. First, top managers may feel overloaded and unable to concentrate if all decisions must go via them. Second, decentralization speeds up decision-making by eliminating the need to convey requests up the hierarchy. Thirdly, it lets experts make choices, improving efficiency. Fourthly, decentralization makes workers who like heading their own departments happy. Finally, it identifies people with good decision-making skills for promotions.

Decentralization may lead to poor coordination and ineffective decision-making. Divisions may make choices that benefit themselves but hurt the company. The head office or board of directors may need to intervene to guarantee department cohesiveness.

Downsizing to cut costs, delayering to gain flexibility, outsourcing non-core operations to specialized firms, offshoring to take advantage of lower labor costs, and implementing shared services to consolidate operations are recent organizational structure trends.

## 9. Formal and Informal

Organizations are formal and informal. Organization procedures manuals and performance reviews purposefully construct and record formal organization. A large part of the organization is informal, including personal goals, group conventions, preferences, rumors, and alliances. The informal organization may considerably affect how people behave and interact; thus, management must understand and control it.

Management knows about informal organizations, but comprehending their dynamics is difficult. Personal goals, connections, and departures from official rules might affect the organization.

## 2: Describe key features of corporate issuers

Following are the key features of corporate issuers.

### Separate legal identity

The corporation is a legal entity separate from its owners. It can enter into a contract, hire and fire employees, and do other related activities. It has certain rights and responsibilities that are separate from those of the owners.

### Separate owners and managers

The owners (shareholders) and the managers of the company are different. The managers (who manage the business) are elected through the shareholders' votes. These managers are called the board of directors.

### Limited liability

The shareholders have limited liability. In case of losses, they can lose up to their share of investment.

### Financing from external sources

The separate identity makes the corporation borrow from external financiers.

### Separate taxation

The corporations are taxed separately from the shareholders. The double taxation concept means the corporation is taxed separately when it earns income. Afterward, when this income is distributed among the shareholders, the shareholders are also required to pay income tax according to their tax circumstances.

### 3: Compare publicly and privately owned corporate issuers

There are two types of limited companies

Private Limited

Public Limited

1. **Private limited companies:** Private companies issue shares through a private placement memorandum, also called an offering memorandum. These shares are only offered to accredited investors with a certain risk tolerance level (due to higher income or higher net worth, etc.). The shares of these private companies are traded in an unregulated market. The

shares of private limited companies are regarded as higher risk than publicly traded companies. Private limited companies may go public via either an Initial Public Offering (IPO), Direct Listing (DL), or acquisition.

1. **Public limited companies:** Public limited companies offer shares to the general public, which are subsequently exchanged on a secondary market (an exchange). These corporations are subject to stricter rules than private limited firms. These firms must provide information to the general public at regular intervals. The data is readily available to the general public and investors.

# Learning Module 2
# Investors and Other Stakeholders

**1: Compare the financial claims and motivations of lenders and shareholders**

**Shareholders:** Shareholders provide equity capital for the firm and hold residual claims of the company's assets after payment of all liabilities. Shareholders can be individuals or institutions who own at least one share in a company. Shareholders want the company to grow, so their equity increases. They are also entitled to dividends.

Shareholders have the voting rights to elect a board of directors and significant other company decisions. This board of directors is the representative of shareholders in the company. The board of directors manages all the affairs of the company through senior management and other staff. So, the shareholders have tremendous power to influence the company matters. Some shareholders have a significant portion of shares and can influence the elections, so they are collectively called controlling shareholders. Other than controlling shareholders, there are minor shareholders who have little power to control or influence the company matters.

All the payments to shareholders are made at the last stage in case of the firm's liquidity or dividend announcement. Before any shareholder gets paid, all the obligations must be fulfilled.

**Creditors:** These are the debt providers to the company in return for interest payments plus the principal amount. The creditors have no voting power so they cannot influence the company's matters. They want the company to generate enough cash flows from main business activities so they get paid according to the plan. Creditors are usually banks and bondholders of the firm.

Creditors hate if a company takes risks, while the shareholders may want high risk with higher expected returns.

The creditors can restrict the firm's activities by using covenants (These are the restrictions imposed by lenders to borrowers to protect lenders' interests, i.e., repayment of debt. Debt covenants reduce the default risk, reducing borrowing costs).

**2: Describe a company's stakeholder groups and compare their interests**

Company's stakeholders: A company's stakeholders are all those with interests in the company. Different stakeholders may or may not have conflicts of interest. The following are the main stakeholders of a firm;

**Shareholders:** Shareholders provide equity capital for the firm and hold residual claims of the company's assets after payment of all liabilities. Shareholders can be individuals or institutions owning at least one company share. Shareholders want the company to grow, so their equity increases. They are also entitled to dividends.

Shareholders have the voting rights to elect a board of directors and major other company decisions. This board of directors is the representative of shareholders in the company. The board of directors manages all the company affairs through senior management and other staff. So, the shareholders have tremendous power to influence the company matters. Some shareholders have major shares and can influence the elections so they are collectively called controlling shareholders. Other than controlling shareholders, some minor shareholders have little power to control or influence the company matters.

All the payments to shareholders are made at the last stage in case of the firm's liquidity or dividend announcement. Before any shareholder gets paid, all the obligations must be fulfilled.

**Creditors:** These are the debt providers to the company in return for interest payments plus the principal amount. The creditors have no voting power, so they cannot influence the company's matters. They want the company to generate enough cash flows from main business activities so they get paid according to the plan. Creditors are usually banks and bondholders of the firm.

Creditors hate if a company takes risks, while the shareholders may want high risk with higher expected returns.

The creditors can restrict the firm's activities by using covenants (These are the restrictions imposed by lenders to borrowers to protect lenders' interests, i.e., repayment of debt. Debt covenants reduce the default risk, so it also lowers borrowing costs.).

**Managers:** Managers and other employees are the people who work for the company for remuneration. They want job security and maximum compensation. Usually, they achieve these two objectives when the company prospers. So they have interests like shareholders. Sometimes, their interests conflict with the shareholders firing a manager is good for the company and shareholders, but that's bad for the employees.

**Board of Directors:** Shareholders elect a board of directors. They manage all the company affairs by hiring other employees (senior management). They are the representatives of the shareholders in the firm.

**Customers:** Customers are the buyers of goods or services of the firm. They want their company to produce high-quality goods/services. They do not have any interest in the financial performance of the firm.

**Regulatory bodies and government:** The regulatory bodies want the company to work according to the law and protect the economy as a whole. The government wants the maximum tax revenues from the firm without hindering its operations. The government has other interests like employment protection, no child labor, environmental effects, etc.

**Suppliers:** These are the firms are the individuals who supply the raw material to the firm. They are short-term creditors, so their interests are like creditors.

**3: Describe environmental, social, and governance factors of corporate issuers considered by investors**

**ESG integration:** While making investment decisions in companies, the investors consider these companies' impact on the environment, society, and governance. The socially responsible and cautious investors avoid all those companies which are affecting negatively (to EGG). This practice is called ESG integration into portfolio planning and construction.

ESG can be divided into the following sub-categories;

*Environmental issues:* Like the increase in pollution, contaminating water, etc.

*Social issues:* Child labor, gender inequality, etc.

*Governance issues:* Bribery, corruption, etc.

For example, avoiding investment in tobacco companies is a common practice.

The investors set some criteria and eliminated all those companies from the list that are using 'bad practices`. This can limit their investable asset, reducing their overall returns. The research on ESG and return suggests mixed results.

The following methods can implement ESG integration;

**Negative screening:** In this method, we exclude some sectors or companies from our investment considerations. These excluded companies can be involved in issues like an increase in pollution, contaminating water, child labor, gender inequality, bribery, corruption, etc.

**Positive screening:** In this method, we only include companies with good ESG-related principles.

**Relative or Best-in-class approach:** In this method, we only include companies with the highest ESG score in the industry.

**Thematic investment:** In this approach, we consider all companies involved in specific ESG goals like energy efficiency and climate change. For example, companies using water and clean energy sources efficiently.

# Learning Module 3
# Corporate Governance: Conflicts, Mechanisms, Risks, and Benefits

**1: Describe the principal-agent relationship and conflicts that may arise between stakeholder groups**

Principal-agent relationship is formed when somebody (the principal) hires someone (the agent) to complete a task in interest of principal. If the interests of agent are different from principal, a conflict of interest is developed. For example, if an employee is not working for the best interests of the shareholder.

**Shareholders and manager/director conflict of interest:** Directors are appointed by the shareholders to maximize the shareholders' equity. The directors may not take some risks that could maximize the equity but are too risky. The board of directors is paid for their performance, and if the company goes down by taking that risk, the board of directors could be blamed. So, they usually avoid risk. In this case, a conflict of interest arises.

The directors and managers usually have more access to the latest information about the company. This is called asymmetry of information.

The board of directors appoints managers who want maximum remuneration and other perks. Their interests may also differ from those of shareholders in certain situations.

**Controlling shareholders and minority shareholders:** The controlling shareholders have the majority of shares, so they are highly influential in company matters. Controlling shareholder can exploit their control and make certain decisions that are not in the best interest of minority shareholders.

**Shareholders and creditors:** The shareholders may want to reinvest the profits or borrow new funds to maximize their wealth, but these two activities are not in the best interests of creditors because the creditors want a smooth flow of cash for debt repayment.

**Customers and shareholders:** Certain activities create a conflict of interest between these two. For example, an increase in product price and reducing the quality of products or services.

**Shareholders and suppliers:** like creditors, the conflict of interest between these two could arise from the same situations.

**Shareholders and regulatory bodies:** The Company can adopt new policies that could defer tax payments or reduce tax payments. These activities are in the best interest of shareholders but conflict with regulatory bodies and the government.

**2: Describe corporate governance and mechanisms to manage stakeholder relationships and mitigate associated risks**

Different stakeholders have different interests. These interests must be identified and prioritized. Stakeholder management means maintaining good relationships with all the stakeholders. This can be done by effective engagement and communication.

The stakeholder management can be different from company to company and country to country. However, the basic guideline is to minimize any potential conflict of interest.

**Stakeholder management components:** There are four components to manage relationships with stakeholders

Legal infrastructure: Legal infrastructure involves the rights and obligations of stakeholders defined by the law.

Contractual infrastructure: This includes the contractual agreement between all the shareholders. The companies generally have more control over contractual infrastructures.

Organizational infrastructure: It includes the company's process, procedures and practices by which it manages the relationships with stakeholders.

<u>Governmental infrastructure:</u> The regulations imposed by the government and its regulatory bodies to manage the rights and obligations of stakeholders.

Different mechanisms to manage stakeholders' relationships are as follows;

**Annual General Meeting (AGM):** Annual general meetings are usually held after the completion of a financial year. The shareholders attend these meetings. They are presented the audited financial statements, the annual growth report and other documents by the management. The shareholders can ask questions about any concerns if they have any. Any individual who has the shares of a company can attend its meetings. The shareholders who cannot attend the meeting can use proxy voting rights. In *proxy voting* a shareholder can assign anybody to use his voting right.

*Extraordinary general meetings* can be called by the shareholders or management whenever there is a need for shareholders' approval to pass a resolution. The typical purposes of extraordinary meetings can include acquisitions, mergers, a material change in corporate governance of the company, etc.

Resolutions can also be of two types: ordinary resolutions and special resolutions.

*Ordinary resolution:* These are of ordinary nature and may include the appointment of an auditor, board of director elections, etc. A simple majority vote cast is required to pass an ordinary resolution.

A special resolution may include issues like acquisitions, mergers, a material change in corporate governance of the company, etc. A two-thirds or three-fourth majority of all cast votes is required to pass a special resolution.

Voting methods also vary. Simple voting means allocating a total number of votes to elect a board member or to pass a resolution. In cumulative voting, the total voting rights increase. Total voting rights in cumulative voting are equal to the number of votes held multiplied by the number of boards of directors. For example, a shareholder has 100 shares, and there are 5 members to be elected. A total of 100 x 5 =500 votes can be cast by that shareholder. In cumulative voting, minority shareholders enjoy a better representation in company matters.

In some cases, the minority shareholders can have special privileges established by the law. These special situations include acquisitions and mergers. This is because these incidents can affect minority shareholders the most.

**3: Describe potential risks of poor corporate governance and stakeholder management and benefits of effective corporate governance and stakeholder management**

**Potential risks of poor corporate governance and stakeholder management:**

- One stakeholder can gain extra advantage over the cost of other stakeholder.
- When the system is not well established the management can make poor decisions that are in their own favor not for all stakeholders
- The legal and regulatory risks increase
- The company's reputation is degraded
- The lower quality products will be produced and the demand will fall.

- A company with a bad reputation struggles with new funds in times of need

- The risk of default increases as the debt obligations would not be paid on time

**Potential benefits of good corporate governance and stakeholder management:**

- The default and legal risk can be reduced
- Good investment and other decision-making
- Ability to raise low-cost capital
- Increase in reputation
- No stakeholder can gain on the cost of others
- The company will be operating optimally so the cost of doing business falls. As a result profitability increases
- Good relations with customers will increase market demand

The internal and external control will be effective

# Learning module 4
# Working Capital and Liquidity

**1: Explain the cash conversion cycle and compare issuers' cash conversion cycles**

**Cash conversion cycle** (or Net Operating cycle) = {(days sales outstanding) + days inventory in hand) – (Number of days of payables)}

It is the time a company takes to turn a product into cash (from cash paid to purchase inventory to receivable to cash collection).

A shorter Cash conversion cycle and Operating cycle means greater liquidity. It should be compared with industry norms. A longer of these two means too much investment is tied up into working capital.

**2: Explain liquidity and compare issuers' liquidity levels**

**Liquidity position of a firm:** It means how a company's current assets are, compared to the current liabilities as a percentage of total assets. The higher the percentage of current assets is, the better. It means the company's ability to generate cash in case of the need to fulfill its short-term requirements.

Liquidity position is measured using Liquidity based ratios:

Measures the firm's ability to meet short-term obligations. However, these ratios must not be considered in isolation. They must be compared with peer groups of companies.

**Current ratio:** = current assets / current Liabilities. It measures how many times a firm has current assets to meet current liabilities. A ratio of 1 or higher is desirable. One drawback of the current ratio is that the makeup of current assets could be very different from company to company. So, the current ratio could be very misleading. For example, if the firm has more inventory and less cash, the current ratio might be greater than one, but this situation is not ideal (as inventory is not considered a great source of finance in the short term).

To cover this flaw, we have **a quick ratio, which considers** more liquid assets. Quick ratio = {Cash + marketable securities + receivables} / Current liabilities.

**Cash ratio=** {cash + marketable securities} / current liabilities.

In addition to liquidity ratios, we also use activity ratios to better understand the companies, which are as follows;

**Receivable turnover ratio:** How efficiently a firm controls receivables is measured by **receivable turnover ratio.**

**Receivable turnover ratio = credit sales/ average receivables.**

This ratio should be closer to industry norms.

One thing that must be remembered here is that whenever we use balance sheet data with income statement or cash flow data in a ratio, the balance sheet figure must be taken as average by adding opening and ending balances and dividing by 2.

**Number of days sales are outstanding or average collection period:** It is the average number of days taken by the customers to pay to the firm.

**No. of days sales outstanding = 365/ receivable turnover**

This ratio should be close to industry norms. If it is too high, it means the firm is not collecting cash easily (inefficiency). A too low this ratio shows a very strict credit policy which might be affecting sales or the firm is collecting cash very efficiently.

**Inventory turnover ratio= Cost of goods sold/ average inventory**

It measures firm's efficiency in inventory management and its processing. It tells how often the firm has sold its inventory completely (theoretically).

**Days inventory in hand = 365/ inventory turnover**

It tells us how many days a firm takes to process its inventory. Again, these (Inventory turnover and Days inventory in hand) should be close to industry norms. A higher inventory turnover ratio means fewer days of inventory in hand. It might indicate a highly effective inventory management, or the company is not holding enough stock and is potentially on the verge of shortages and falling sales revenue. Analysts must see revenue growth to assess the explanation. A higher (or the same as industry) growth with high turnover means effective inventory management and vice versa. A lower inventory turnover means a higher number of days of inventory in hand, which may indicate that there is too much capital tied up and high processing time. It means inventory could be getting obsolete. The cost of goods sold may not be according to current circumstances.

**Payable turnover ratio = purchases/ average payables:** It means how many times a company pays its payables completely (theoretically).

**Number of days of payables= 365/ payable turnover ratio**

These two should be close to industry norms. With a relatively higher payables turnover (which would mean a relatively lower number of days payables are outstanding), the company might not be effectively taking advantage of credit facilities made available to them, or they might be taking advantage of early payment discounts. We must look at the liquidity ratios to get a proper understanding. If a company has better liquidity ratios but higher days payable (lower payable turnover), it means they are taking advantage of available credit facilities. If the liquidity position is bad with lower payable turnover, they might be having trouble with cash generation.

**Working capital turnover = Total sales/ average working capital.** Working capital is the difference between current assets and current liabilities.

It tells us how efficiently the company turns its working capital investment into sales revenue. It indicates how much revenue the company generates per dollar of working capital investment. For example, if the working capital turnover is 5, it means for every dollar of working capital, we generate five dollars of sales revenue. A zero or negative of this ratio is not useable.

## 3: Describe issuers' objectives and compare methods for managing working capital and liquidity

### Objectives:

Companies need to manage liquidity and working capital to meet short-term obligations. Liquidity is the ability to generate cash at a time of need with minimum or no cost. Firms in industries need different liquidity requirements, and they approximate their day-to-day needs for that purpose.

Working capital is the difference between current assets and current liabilities.

It tells us how efficiently the company is turning its working capital investment into sales revenue. It indicates how much revenue the company is generating per dollar of working capital investment. For example, if the working capital turnover is 5, it means for every dollar of working capital, we generate five dollars of sales revenue. A zero or negative of this ratio is not useable.

There are two broad types of liquidity resources however they can vary from company to company; primary sources and secondary sources.

**Primary sources:** The use of primary sources of liquidity does not affect the company's normal course of business. The major primary sources of liquidity can include

- Balance in bank
- Cash received from customers
- Line of credit from a bank
- Line of credit from company suppliers
- Account receivables
- Selling of short-term investments
- Effective cash flow management

**Secondary sources:** Using secondary sources of liquidity changes the normal course of business. It can change the capital structure of the company and its operations. The use of secondary sources can be a sign of poor management. Secondary sources of liquidity may include

- Negotiated or re-negotiated debt
- Selling current (inventory) and long-lived assets
- Filing bankruptcy

**Factors affecting liquidity position**

Generally, early cash-ins and slow cash-outs are considered a good sign of cash management, but it can vary from company to company and industry to industry. Usually, the cash flow must match the industry's traditions.

Broadly speaking, two factors weaken a company's liquidity position: the drags on liquidity and pulls on liquidity.

*Drags on liquidity:* Any factor that reduces the inflows of cash comes under this heading. Uncollected receivables, increase in bad debts, higher discounts on sales, inventory getting obsolete (because it takes more time to sell), and higher cost of borrowings (tight credit) are "drags on liquidity."

*Pulls on liquidity*: All factors that pull out the cash from the company are pulls on liquidity. These factors are

Early payment

Reducing and or limiting the credit lines

**Working capital management**

There are two broad approaches to managing working capital

1. Aggressive approach
2. Conservative approach
3. Moderate approach

**1. Aggressive approach**

In an aggressive approach, companies minimize the surplus liquid assets like cash and inventory, etc., and mostly rely on short-term financing to meet day-to-day needs. This approach is useful when you aim to earn profits but sacrifice liquidity. This approach is usually adopted in stable economic environments with fewer future uncertainties. However, this approach is risky, and if the interest rate rises and the short-term financing is unavailable, the companies will face difficulties.

## 1.  Conservative approach

In this approach, companies maintain higher liquid assets and cash. These companies use long-term financing instead of short-term financing for working capital requirements. These companies usually face fewer difficulties in case of economic disruptions. Because they do not rely heavily on any changes in interest rates and other financial indicators, however, this approach restricts investment and short-term financing opportunities.

## 1.  Moderate approach

This strategy is the best of the two approaches. In this strategy, companies use short-term financing for short-term assets and long-term financing for long-term assets. It reduces the financing costs in comparison to an aggressive approach. This approach is useful when you have stable cash inflows and working capital requirements are also predictable with high accuracy. This approach reduces the interest rate risk but also reduces the short-term financing and investment opportunities. Refinancing permanent assets in an era of economic disruptions is also challenging.

# Learning module 5
# Capital Investments and Capital Allocation

**1: Describe types of capital investment**

A capital investment (capital project) is a project whose lifespan is more than one year. Capital investment (capital projects) evaluation is a process or method companies use to evaluate capital projects. Capital allocation helps in the decision-making of which project to choose and which project to leave, based on cost-benefit analysis.

Capital allocation is critical, and the finance manager should take good care in this process. Capital projects can include purchasing costly machinery, installing new plants, etc.

Typical capital investments include;

- **Replacement projects:** These projects can include replacing old machinery, plant and equipment, replacement of machinery, etc.
- **Expansion projects:** Increase in size of the company.
- **New product:** Launching new products.
- **Regulatory projects:** The projects required by government or regulatory bodies.
- **Other projects:** Like research and development projects whose cash flows are not certain.

**2: Describe the capital allocation process, calculate net present value (NPV), internal rate of return (IRR), and return on invested capital (ROIC), and contrast their use in capital allocation**

**Capital Allocation** is a process or method companies use to evaluate capital projects. Capital allocation helps decide which project to choose and which to leave based on cost-benefit analysis.

A capital project is a project whose lifespan is more than one year.

Capital allocation is very important, and the finance manager should take good care in this process. Capital projects can include purchasing costly machinery, installing new plants, etc.

Steps of the capital allocation process

1. **Idea generating:** Generating good ideas is the first and vital step.
2. **Analyze individual proposals:** Gather maximum information about each idea. Evaluate and forecast the cash inflows and outflows and their timings and profitability.
3. **Plan capital allocation:** Prioritize and organize all projects within the firm's strategies.
4. **Assessing, monitoring, and post-auditing:** Examining how the project performs, related to forecasts.

**Capital investment methods**

**Net present value:** Net present value is the present value of all future cash flows minus initial investment.

The discount rate is the cost of capital adjusted for the risk.

Formula

$$NPV = \text{Initial investment} + \frac{\text{Cash flow1}}{(1+r)^1} + \frac{\text{Cash flow2}}{(1+r)^2} + \ldots\ldots \frac{\text{Cash flow 'n}}{(1+r)^n}$$

or

$$NPV = \sum_{t=0}^{n} \frac{CFt}{(1+r)^t}$$

Whereas;

"t" is the time of the project or the point of time of each cash flows

CF is the cash flow (after tax)

"r" is the required rate of return or cost of capital.

With independent projects

The projects with NPV >0 can be accepted because this project will increase the shareholders' wealth.

The projects with NPV <0 can be rejected because this project will decrease the shareholders' wealth.

Projects with NPV=0 can be accepted or rejected because they will not impact shareholders' wealth.

**Advantages of NPV:**

- NPV gives a clear measure.
- NPV takes into consideration the size of the investment.
- The calculation of NPV is simple.
- NPV is calculated using cash flows rather than net earnings (net of depreciation).

**Disadvantages of NPV:**

The main disadvantage of the net present value method is that it needs some guesswork regarding the firm's cost of capital. This method is very sensitive to inputs.

**IRR:** *IRR is the discount rate that makes the net present value of all the cash flows equal to zero.*

$$NPV = \frac{Cash\ flow1}{(1+irr)^1} + \frac{Cash\ flow2}{(1+irr)^2} + \ldots \ldots \frac{Cash\ flow\ n}{(1+irr)^n} = 0$$

Or

$$NPV = \sum_{t=0}^{n} \frac{CFt}{(1+irr)^t} = 0$$

Solve for "irr".

With independent projects

The projects with IRR >"r" can be accepted because this project will increase the shareholders' wealth.

Projects with IRR >"r" can be rejected because they will decrease the shareholders' wealth.

Projects with IRR >"r" can be accepted or rejected because they will not have any impact on shareholders' wealth.

"r" is the cost of capital.

**Limitations of IRR**

- It disregards the true monetary worth of comparable investments.
- Sometimes, we get multiple or no IRR.

_Limitations of NPV and IRR:_ These methods cannot be used when future cash flows are uncertain. These measures are also very sensitive to cash inflows and outflows.

**NPV profile:** NPV profile means the graph of NPV and discount rate. It shows different NPVS at different discount rates.

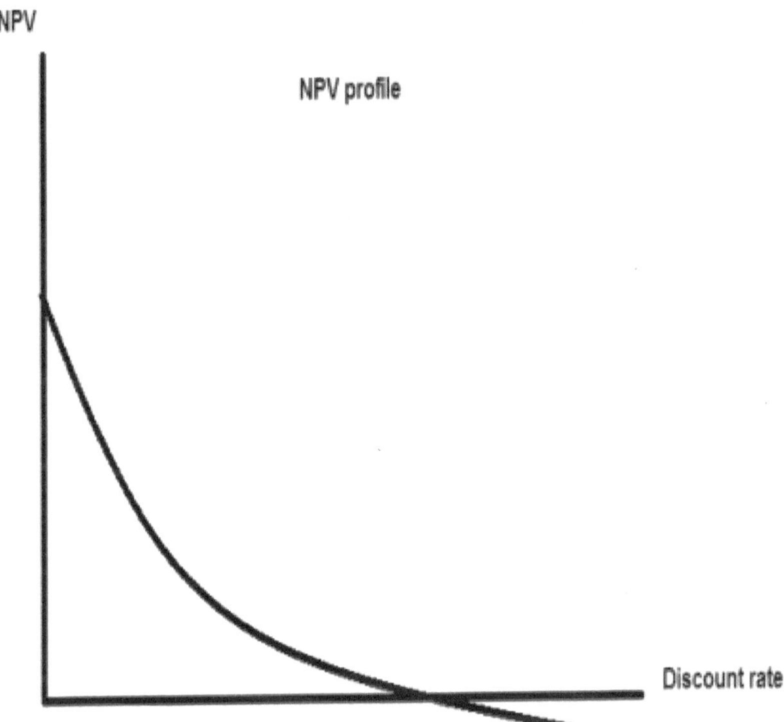


When the discount rate is zero, the line hits the y-axis. When the NPV is zero, the line hits the X-axis.

The NPV and IRR both are good and produce the same conclusions about two independent projects.

When the projects are mutually exclusive, both of these measures may take us to different rankings and conclusions. One project's NPV might be greater than another, but the IRR of another project might be greater than the project with a higher NPV. In this case, generally, the NPV is preferred over IRR conclusions.

This difference in ranking may be the result of different timings of the cash flows between the two projects.

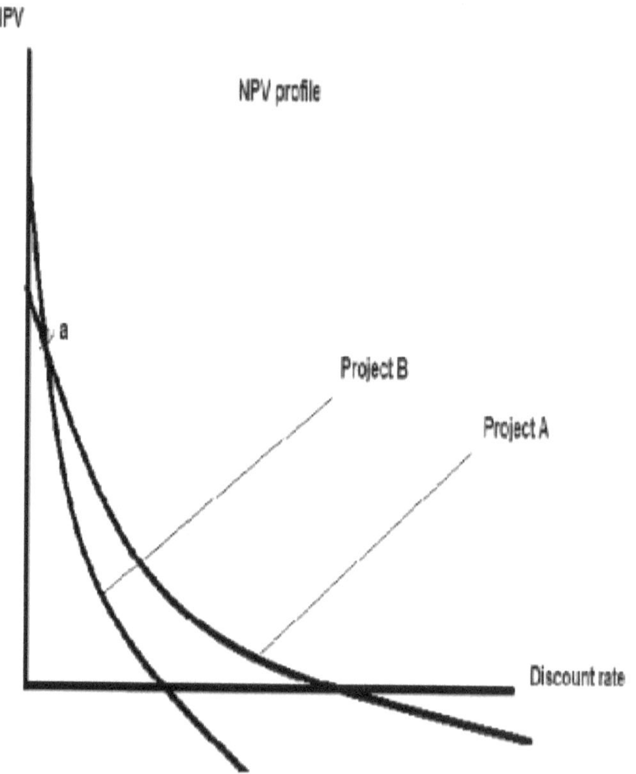



Sometimes, we come up with the same NPV for two projects at a specific discount rate, as shown in the above graph. At point "a," the NPV of both projects is the same (the point is called crossover). This happens due to differences in the timings of cash flows. Indeed, project A has better NPV at most discount rates. Project A is better if your discount rate is higher than point a's discount rate.

**Comparison of NPV and IRR:** NPV is preferred over IRR because it is more reliable in cases of zero or multiple IRR. However, the NPV does not consider the size of the project. A project of 100 million with an NPV of $500 might not be as good as another project of 50 million with an NPV of $500.

The IRR method, however, gives us the per-dollar return. But the IRR can be zero or there can be more than IRR.

The NPV and IRR both are good and produce the same conclusions about two independent projects.

When the projects are mutually exclusive, both of these measures may take us to different rankings and conclusions. One project's NPV might be greater than another, but the IRR of another project might be greater than the project with a higher NPV. In this case, generally, the NPV is preferred over IRR conclusions.

This difference in ranking may be a result of

- Different timings of the cash flows between two projects
- Difference in sizes of two projects

We always go with the NPV method in case of conflict because the NPV implicitly assumes that the inflows can be reinvested at the existing discount rate (a reality-based assumption).

The assumption behind IRR is that we can reinvest at IRR. This is a less realistic assumption because if the firm could reinvest at IRR, then the discount rate used in NPV should be equal to IRR.

If a project has multiple cash inflows and outflows, its IRR could be zero or more than one. In this case, the IRR method fails. This type of project can still be profitable. In this case, as we have already mentioned, we prefer the NPV conclusion.

**ROIC:** Return on invested capital or return on capital invested (also called return on capital employed ROCE), It is a way for management to gauge the return on investment of their whole capital.

ROIC= Operating profit after tax / Average invested capital

While average invested capital = average long-term liabilities plus equity.

It indicates how successfully a firm uses its money and whether or not it generates value for its shareholders via investment. It should be at least as high as the company's cost of capital. ROIC shows total growth while the above other measures show annual growth. Moreover, this measure can be calculated more effectively and quickly due to readily available data.

### 3: Describe principles of capital allocation and common capital allocation pitfalls

Capital allocation must follow the following principles;

- Decisions on capital budgeting are based on cash flows and not only accounting concepts like net income. Moreover, intangibles are only considered when they cause a cash flow.
- **Timings of cash flows:** Timings of cash flows are very important. The managers should take good care to forecast the timings of each cash flow. This is mainly because early inflows and delayed outflows are better than early outflows and delayed inflows due to the time value of money.
- **Cash flows are based on opportunity costs:** Opportunity costs are those incomes that will be gone if we undertake a project.
- Cash flows should be considered **after deduction of taxes**
- **Financing cost is ignored** in capital budgeting because it is already being reflected in the required rate of return (rrr).
- **Cash flows are not considered net income** because net income means revenues minus all costs, but costs are not deducted from cash inflows.


Some basic concepts related to capital budgeting;

**Sunk cost:** It is the cost that is already made and cannot be recovered. Sometimes, it is incurred before even starting a project like consultation costs.

**Incremental cash flows:** The cash flows if we have undertaken a project. Incremental cash flows = cash flows after the decision about a project has been undertaken minus the cash flows before that decision.

**Externalities:** The effect of investment on other projects of the same firm's cash flows. When a new project decision has a negative impact on another ongoing project, it is called cannibalism. For example, a company introduces a new car, and existing customers of the old model move towards a new car.

In capital budgeting, these externalities must be considered.

**Conventional cash flows:** It is the series of cash flows in which there is an initial cash outflow, and then there are cash inflows.

**Unconventional cash flows:** These cash flows do not follow the patterns of conventional cash flows. There might be initial inflow and then outflows. The direction of cash flows can change from time to time.

# Companies can fall prey to the following common pitfalls while allocating capital

- Under/overestimation of the cost of capital. Under or overestimating the cost of capital can change the value of a project change dramatically.
- Not considering qualitative factors like customer loyalty, staff loyalty, etc.
- Not considering macroeconomic variables.
- Biasness of managers towards a specific project.
- Investing in projects that do not align with the company's long-term goals while focusing on short-term earnings.
- Depending on the IRR method alone.
- The use of appropriate accounting methods to make projects attractive or unattractive.
- Whether appropriate or not, consider sunk cost and opportunity cost.

**4: Describe types of real options relevant to capital investments**

**Options:** Options are derivatives that give the right (not obligation) to its holder to buy or sell a commodity (or any other underlying) at a future date at a specific price. Some options are OTC while others are exchange traded.

**Real Options:** Real options give the right (not obligation) to its holder to take a business initiative (or any business transaction) at a future date at a specific price. These options are called real because they involve real (tangible) assets like the installation of a new plant or machinery or construction of a factory, etc.

Real options usually have the following (but not limited to) types

1. **Option to expand:** It enables the companies to spend more money to develop their operations, i.e., in other areas. This option is also known as the Growth Option. This expansion may make the project look better by improving NPV. For example, a US company wanted to expand its business in India, but the inflows from the initial investment in India did not seem promising because of changing political and environmental issues. The company can buy a real investment to buy a property to establish a factory in India and save its future.

2. **Option to Abandon:** This option permits the investor to halt or abandon the project to obtain its salvage value. It allows the investor to exit the project and helps limit losses.

3. **Option to wait:** Companies use this option to postpone a decision until later or resume work on the project when conditions improve. This option is also known as the Timing Option or the Option to Delay.

4. **Option to Contract:** If the external variables are not favorable, a company can stop or shut down a project at any moment in the future, i.e., due to political unrest.

5. **Option to Redeploy:** This option allows a company to redeploy its resources to another project if the original project is no longer feasible or if a new, more lucrative opportunity arises.

# There are four methods used to evaluate capital projects with real options

1. Discounted cash flow method: In this model, all the future expected cash flows are discounted to get the present value of a project. These cash flows can include all cash in and outflows. If the present value is positive or higher than any other available project, it means the project is viable.
2. Using NPV minus the cost of an option
3. Option pricing model
4. Decision tree

# Learning Module 6
# Capital Structure

**1: Calculate and interpret the weighted-average cost of capital for a company**

Weighted average cost of capital is the cost to raise capital. Companies have different types of funds for their capital needs. They can borrow from banks and from investors (bonds) by issuing preferred stock and issuing common equity. The weighted average cost of capital is the aggregate cost of all these types of funds.

WACC= Wd*Kd(1-t) + Wps*Kps + Wce*Kce

Whereas

*Wd means the proportionate weight of debt in the total funds*

*Kd is the rate of interest to be paid to the lenders. That's the yield to maturity of existing debt.*

*Wps is the weight of preferred stocks in total funds*

*Kps is the cost of preferred stocks*

*Kps is the cost of issuing common stock*

*Wce is the weight of common equity*

*Kce is the cost of common equity which investors are required to invest in the firm. This is the most difficult one to calculate*

Usually, the debt is tax deductible, so we have used (1-t) with Kd.

That means after-tax cost of debt.

So the WACC is nothing but a weighted mean.

The WACC is the rate at which a company can raise funds. So this is also the discount rate at which capital budgeting should be calculated. If IRR is greater than WACC, then the project is viable; otherwise not.

WACC is also an opportunity cost for the company. Imagine if the company had not raised these funds to finance certain assets; it could have saved this cost.

**2: Explain factors affecting capital structure and the weighted-average cost of capital**

Optimal capital structure is the mix of debt and equity, which minimizes the cost of capital. Optimal capital structure is ideal, and every firm wants to attain it. However, every firm has its own limitations in reaching this ideal situation. The capital structure depends on the following factors;

- Capital structure policies and targets
- Capital investment financing
- Market conditions
- Asymmetric information

**Capital structure policies and targets**

The appropriate mix of debt and equity is achieved according to a company's targeted capital structure. Although not all organizations require capital structure policies, they are critical for frequent borrowers due to the dangers associated with excessive leverage. Regulators may mandate a capital structure mix in specific businesses.

*Debt rating:* Firms' debts are rated by independent organizations. Debt ratings tend to fall as the firm borrows more (or issues more debt). As debt ratings fall, they become more risky, and lenders want a higher interest rate (return) on their lending. As a result, firms borrow less because their cost of capital is on the rise.

*Market value vs book value:* While the market value of equity and debt is used to determine the ideal capital structure, for the following reasons, company capital structure targets frequently use book value instead:

Market values can fluctuate dramatically, while it has no effect on the optimal level of borrowing.

Management is most concerned with the amount and types of capital invested by the company, rather than the company itself.

The capital structure policy ensures that management has the ability to borrow quickly and at a low cost. Lenders and rating agencies calculate debt and equity based on book values.

### Financing Capital Investments

Investment spending is typically linked to critical financing decisions. Management will examine the characteristics and requirements of the asset or investment at the time of financing, as well as the company's overall capital structure after the investment has been made.

Assets like real estate are good for leverage because they are easy to market, generate cash, and are generally regarded as solid collateral by lenders. Lenders typically ignore businesses with more intangible assets.

Foreign investments are usually made in debt to hedge currency risk, reduce taxes, and still produce revenues.

### Market conditions

Market conditions play a huge role in making capital decisions. Companies watch the current market price of their shares and interest rates on their loans when deciding when, how much, and what type of capital to issue.

### Asymmetric information and signaling

The management has more information about the company affairs, and there are chances of conflict of interest between lenders and borrowers; the lenders demand a higher return on capital with a higher level of information asymmetry.

According to the pecking order theory, managers prefer financing from internally generated funds, debt, and equity. Companies are more likely to issue equity if they believe their stock is overvalued.

Agency cost: The companies are managed by the agents (the managers) but owned by shareholders (principals). The agency cost arises as a result of a conflict of interest between the principal and agents. Managers usually want executive flights and luxurious lunches, which are costly for the shareholders. Agency theory states that when a company uses more leverage, the managers are less likely to use the money foolishly.

A company's life cycle is an integral part of the strategic analysis because its stage impacts its competitiveness, growth, capital requirements, and, ultimately, profits. As the stage changes, the above characteristics also change, so the company should be analyzed on an ongoing basis. There are five stages of an industry;

1.  **Start-up:** This is when a company has just started. This stage has the following characteristics;

- Slow growth
- High prices
- Low volumes and sales
- High failure risk
- Need for huge investment
- Negative capital flows (outflows)
- Limited or no debt availability

1.  **Growth stage:** Customers start discovering the product in this stage. There is less competition, but the threat of new entry is imminent. The following are the characteristics of this stage:

- Falling prices,
- Rapid increase in demand,
- Increase in profitability
- Minimum competition
- Medium-level business risk
- Somewhat cash inflows
- Limited debt available
- Cost of debt is less than as compared to start-up stage

1.  **Mature:**

- Little or no growth
- Consolidation of firms into oligopoly (superior firms will get more market share)
- High barriers to entry
- Stable profits and pricing
- Higher cash inflows
- Low risk of failure
- Less cost of debt
- More debt is available

**Capital-intensive vs capital-light businesses**

Some businesses are naturally capital-intensive, so regardless of stage, they burn colossal capital and mostly rely on debt. Oil exploration and auto manufacturing are some capital-intensive industries.

On the other hand, some businesses are light-capital by nature. They don't have to rely on huge fixed investments. Software development companies are an example. They usually do not rely on debt, and they do not need huge fixed investments. They also produce positive cash flows regardless of their stage.

**Cyclical industries:** Companies in cyclical industries vary in their cash inflows and outflows and tend not to follow the company's staged-based capital structure. Tyre manufacturers, the Auto industry, and mining companies are some examples of cyclicals.

**3: Explain the Modigliani–Miller propositions regarding capital structure**

**Capital structure:** Capital structure of a company is the mix of its debt and equity which have used to finance its operations and growth.

Capital structure is maintained in a way so the value of the company is maximized while minimizing its weighted average cost of capital (WACC).

$$WACC = \left(\frac{E}{V} * Re\right) + \left(\frac{D}{V} * Rd(1 - t)\right)$$

**Where:**

E=Market value of the firm's equity

D=Market value of the firm's debt

V=E+D

Re=Cost of equity

Rd=Cost of debt

t=Corporate tax rate

**Modigliani–Miller propositions**

Modigliani–Miller proposed that the value of a firm becomes independent of its capital structure with certain assumptions. If these assumptions are fulfilled then the value of firm cannot be changed by changing the capital structure of the company. These assumptions are;

1. Investors have homogeneous expectations about future cash flows.
2. All investors can lend and borrow at a risk-free rate.
3. Managers of the company always act to maximize the shareholders' equity.
4. The capital market is perfect. There is no transaction cost, no bankruptcy, and the same information is available to every investor.
5. Financial decisions are made independently.

These assumptions are unrealistic but make the situation easy to understand. Then they gradually eliminate these assumptions to understand the real world situation.

**Proposition of irrelevance: Without taxes the capital structure is irrelevant**

MM model says the market value is unaffected by its capital structure when there is no tax involved. It means the capital structure does not play any role in the market value of a firm without taxes. The MM model says that enterprises have two basic sources of funding: stock and debt. While each method of funding has its own set of advantages and disadvantages, the end result is the same: a company distributes its cash flows to investors, regardless of the funding source used. Investors can buy into or sell out of a firm's cash flows at any time if they have access to the same financial markets.

$$WACC = \left(\frac{E}{V} * Re\right) + \left(\frac{D}{V} * (Rd)\right)$$

**Proposition 2: Without taxes, higher leverage increases the cost of equity.**

According to MM Proposition 1, the value of the company remains unchanged or constant when the capital structure changes. As a result, The WAAC must remain the same with changes in capital structure. As the company utilizes more debt, the risk increases, and the cost of equity must rise.

According to MM Proposition II, the increased cost of equity must perfectly offset the increased usage of lower-cost loans.

**MM proposition with corporate tax:** As the corporate taxes are deductible from table income by an amount equal to (1-marginal tax rate), the value of a leveraged firm is greater than unleveraged firm

VL >VU

VL= Value of leverage firm

VU= Vale of unleveraged firm

The cost of the capital equation becomes as follows;

$$WACC = \left(\frac{E}{V} * Re\right) + \left(\frac{D}{V} * Rd(1 - t)\right)$$

Modigliani and Miller show that if r0 reflects the cost of equity for an all-equity company, the cost of equity for the same company with debt is:

$$WACC = r0 + (r0 - rd)(1 - t)\left(\frac{D}{V}\right)$$

**Criticism on MM propositions**

- Lending and borrowing rate differences
- There is always transaction cost involved
- In financial distress, the cost of borrowing increases, which reduces the profitability and consequently further increases the cost of borrowing for the firm.
- There is always asymmetric information
- There may be a conflict of interest between the manager of the firm, who wants more perks like jet and dining out, while it may not be in the best interests of the shareholders. There are also some monitoring costs involved.

## 4: Describe optimal and target capital structures

Optimal capital structure is the mix of debt and equity which minimizes the cost of capital. Optimal capital structure is ideal, and every firm wants to attain it. However, every firm has its own limitations in reaching this ideal situation.

### Targeted Capital structure

The management can explicitly disclose the weighted average cost of capital. This explicitly disclosed weight is the targeted capital structure for the firm. If the targeted capital structure is not explicitly disclosed, then, an analyst can use the current weight of the capital structure as the targeted capital structure.

Another way to determine targeted capital structure is using the industry average.

If there is a particular trend in capital structure, for example, the decreasing weight of debt and increasing weight of preferred stocks, this trend can be used to estimate targeted capital structure.

Always remember to use the current market value of capital structure while quantifying the capital.

To find out the WACC, we first need to calculate the weight of each part of the capital. For example, if a company has three sources of capital, shared equity, preferred equity, and debt, the weight of each can be calculated as

Weight of debt $(Wd)=$

$$Wd = \frac{\text{market value of debt}}{(\text{market value of debt + market value of common equity + market value of preferred equity})}$$

Similarly

Weight of common equity $(Wc)$

$$Wc = \frac{\text{market value of common equity}}{(\text{market value of debt + market value of common equity + market value of preferred equity})}$$

Weight of preferred equity $(Wp)$

$$Wp = \frac{\text{market value of preferred equity}}{(\text{market value of debt + market value of common equity + market value of preferred equity})}$$

WACC (targeted) $= Wd + Wc + Wp$

# Learning module 7
# Business Models

**1: Describe key features of business models**

It is imperative to have a well-defined business model in order to comprehend the organization's strategy, operations, and target market. Many companies adhere to certain established business models, such as manufacturing and retailers, with minor modifications as necessary. Additionally, innovations and business developments have resulted in the emergence of new and innovative business models, as well as changes in business environments. It is imperative for the analyst to comprehend the business model in order to gain a comprehensive understanding of a company's strengths and weaknesses. Annual reports should provide details about the business model.

A well-defined business model includes the following components;

- Who are the company`s customers,
- What the company is offering,
- What are the distribution channels,
- Pricing strategies, and
- The company`s resources.

Features of the business model

1. **Who** are the customers: The target customer base, whether it be a business (B2B) or a consumer (B2C), should be explicitly identified in a business model. It is necessary to establish the target geographical area, product category, and industry-specific segmentations and identify potential risks and market opportunities.

2. **What:** It should clearly identify the products/services that a

firm provides and how they vary from rivals. What are the demands that the product/services meet, and who are the closest competitors? What are the elements that influence consumers' purchasing choices, such as price, product efficacy, and attractiveness?

3. **How (channels):** How the firm reaches its clients, sales, marketing, distribution, etc. Certain companies conduct certain services internally, while others outsource them. Channel strategy also includes assets such as warehouses, retailers, shops, dealers, and franchises. The choice of channel impacts cost, risk, and profitability.

## Channel strategies

Traditional channel strategy: In this strategy, finished goods are sent from producer to wholesaler, to retailer, and to the customers. This is a good channel for the physical goods.

Direct sales channel: Direct sales: Companies with their own sales team can eliminate suppliers and dealers in direct sales methods. This business route approach is common in the pharmacy industry, as well as in B2B business models.

Omni channel strategy: In this strategy, both direct and traditional channels are employed concurrently. For instance, a consumer may order a product online and deliver it to their doorstep or the nearest pickup location.

1. **How much (pricing strategy):** A business model should clearly explain the pricing strategy of the firm, especially in relation to its competitors. Some firms are price takers (less or no pricing power), while others are price setters. Pricing strategies like premium pricing, parity, or discounts can be offered.

There are two types of pricing models.

Value-based and cost-based

Value-based models charge the price depending on the value customers are getting. For example, a house appliances manufacturer may charge premium prices because their products are highly energy efficient.

Cost-Based model: in this model, companies charge prices in addition to their manufacturing cost.

Price discrimination

It is a strategy of the firm to charge different prices to different customers. The customers can be different in any form, like different geographical areas, different income levels, etc. Price discrimination is used to maximize total revenues. Several strategies are used for price discrimination, like dynamic pricing (prices are charged based on the time of purchase), Tiered pricing (prices depend on the number of goods purchased), auction, and reverse auction. Product bundling, optional product pricing, the high price of assemblies (Razor blade pricing), freemium (free up to a certain level, usually digital products), penetrating the market, hidden revenues model, subscriptions, and leasing are some common pricing strategies.

1. **Value proposition:** the unique characteristic attracts the targeted customers. This is also an essential part of the business model.

2. **Structure of organization and its capabilities:** What is the organization's structure, and how will this structure provide

value to the customers? What are the assets and liabilities of the firm, and are these resources sufficient, or does the firm need more resources?

3. Profitability: The business model should clearly express how the firm is going to earn profit. What are the profit margins, and what are the per unit profit and per unit costs?

## 2: Describe various types of business models

Business models vary from industry to industry and the type of products being offered.

Physical goods-producing firms can have manufacturing, wholesalers, Retailers,

Suppliers of raw materials, components, equipment, and services.

The companies that provide services can be business-to-business (B2B) models or business-to-consumer (B2C). Some business models belong to specific industries like insurance, brokerages, and investment services providers.

### Innovations and business models

The business models can also be innovated or adapted by new innovations. New businesses, primarily digital product providers, operate under business models that are not location-specific, and outsourcing, marketing, and networking have become more accessible and advantageous.

### E-commerce business models

The business model is under the e-commerce model when sales are made through the Internet.

Marketplace business: In this model, the firm develops a network of buyers and or sellers without owning products, i.e., ALIBABA.

Affiliate marketing:

Aggregators: These are just like the marketplace, but they remarket the products or services using their own brands.

### Platform business models

Platform business models are enterprises that link a large number of customers and sellers for short-term buying and selling or long-term interactions, such as creating social ties and working together to achieve a shared objective. These platforms establish rules while facilitating interactions and networks.

Traditional linear business models produce value by transforming raw resources into finished things and selling them to consumers; platform models do this by linking people. Facebook and Uber are some examples of platform models.

### Crowdsourcing Business Models

Users can directly contribute to the value of a product. In crowdfunding, groups of people work together, use the same product, and voluntarily add and contribute. Open-source games are a good example.

### Hybrid business model

As the name implies, the hybrid model combines a platform model with a linear model.

### Other business models

Franchising: The main firm links certain distributors and dealers, and sales are processed via them.

Licensing agreement: Some corporations make things under the name of another company and pay royalties for them.

Contract manufacturers: Also known as private labels. One firm produces items that are sold by another company.

# Don't miss out!

Visit the website below and you can sign up to receive emails whenever M. Imran Ahsan publishes a new book. There's no charge and no obligation.

https://books2read.com/r/B-A-ZWUK-ESTFB

**BOOKS 2 READ**

Connecting independent readers to independent writers.

Did you love *CFA 2026: Level 1 corporate Issuers*? Then you should read *CFA 2025: Level 1 Fixed Income*[1] by M. Imran Ahsan!

If you want to learn CFA easily and with less time, you have the right book. If you think Fixed income is diffcult, just read this book. It will change your perception.

Many books are available in the market for the same purpose and they are good. The main quality of this book which distinguishes it from others is this book covers whole syllabus in very precise and comprehensive manner. This book makes difficult concepts easy and understandable.

We believe in simplicity and conciseness. This book is a complete and a comprehensive guide with simple language.

---

1. https://books2read.com/u/4NL1RW

2. https://books2read.com/u/4NL1RW

You can learn the complete Fixed Income material in just one week with the help of this book.

# Also by M. Imran Ahsan

**ACCA**
ACCA: Business & Technology

**CFA level 1**
CFA 2026: Level 1 corporate Issuers
CFA Level 1 Financial Statement Analysis
CFA level 1: 2025 Equity Investments
CFA 2025: Level 1 Fixed Income
Economics for CFA 2024: level 1 in just one week
CFA Level 1: Derivatives and Alternative Investments
CFA 2025: level 1 Portfolio management

**Investment series**
Corporate Finance: A Beginner's Guide
Fixed Income Securities: A Beginner's Guide to Understand, Invest and
Evaluate Fixed Income Securities

**Personal Finance**

Side Hustle Success: Unlock Your Earning Potential

# About the Author

I am a PhD scholar and is a university lecturer for more than 11 years. I have been teaching Finance and Economics at various levels.

As an instructor I believe in simplicity, comprehensivity and in conciseness. I believe in smart kind of hard work. It means you should use your time efficiently to achieve optimal goals with limited time and efforts.